TRAINS

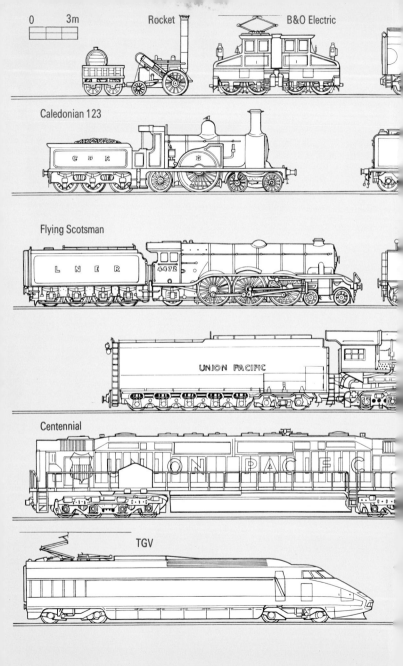

0   3m   Rocket   B&O Electric

Caledonian 123
G & R

Flying Scotsman
L N E R   4472

UNION PACIFIC

Centennial
UNION PACIFIC

TGV

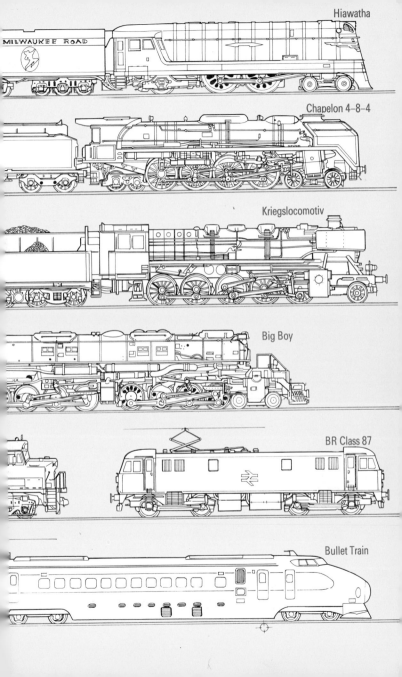

Hiawatha

MILWAUKEE ROAD

Chapelon 4–8–4

Kriegslocomotiv

Big Boy

BR Class 87

Bullet Train

Contents

TRAINS

By Jacquetta Megarry and Keir Bloomer

Editor: Jacqui Bailey
Designer: David Jefferis

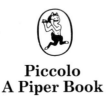

Piccolo
A Piper Book

Early Trains

In 1804 the world's first working steam **locomotive** ran along the rails of a Welsh mining track. It hauled ten tonnes of iron, and about 70 people, who had unofficially climbed on board. The journey of nearly 16 kilometres took 4 hours and 5 minutes and won its builder, Richard Trevithick, a bet of 500 guineas (£505 sterling in gold coins).

Below: The world's first working steam locomotive.

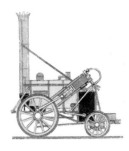

Early steam locomotives: Robert Stephenson's *Rocket* (left) and Marc Seguin's locomotive (right).

Steam trains were not an instant success, however. It was 20 years before the steam train *Locomotion* opened the world's first public railway. The Stockton and Darlington Railway in north-east England opened in 1825, with *Locomotion* hauling 38 wagons of **freight** and 600 passengers. Although its top speed was only about 11 km/h, the train was led by a man on horseback carrying a red flag to warn people of its speed.

Locomotion was designed by George Stephenson and improved on previous steam engine designs. However, the engine was still slow and heavy, and it was mainly used to haul coal trucks. Passenger trains were still horse-drawn. So when a new company was formed to build a passenger railway between Liverpool and Manchester, its directors held a grand competition to find a better engine.

Five locomotives competed in the Rainhill trials of 1829, but only Robert Stephenson's *Rocket* completed the course and met all the conditions. *Rocket*'s success was mainly due to its improved **boiler** design, which gave it a top speed of 47 km/h.

In the same year, Marc Seguin built the first successful French steam locomotive. These faster, more reliable engines made people see that steam railways could be a serious form of transport.

Before Steam

Railways existed long before steam engines. Before 800 BC, the Assyrians had found that it was easier and safer to drive their carts along the ruts made in the mud by previous cartwheels. Later, they paved the roads and made the 'rutways' permanent. These rutways were the ancestors of early modern **tramways**.

Around 500 BC, the Greeks made 'stoneways' by cutting parallel grooves in stone paving blocks. These helped people, horses or mules to pull heavy loads. You can still see these early tramways today in the paved streets of Pompeii in Italy.

In the 16th century, people in Alsace in France built wooden rails in coal mines. The coal was carried from the coal-face in small trucks. Because the rails were raised above the ground, the wheels needed **flanges** to stop them slipping off the rails (see diagram). A similar style of wagon from a Transylvanian gold mine has been preserved in a museum in Berlin.

Iron Rails

Mine railways began to spread through Europe. Wheels glide along rails much more smoothly than along a bumpy road, so a person or horse can pull a greater load. But wooden rails wear out quickly. Then, in the 18th century, iron became cheaper and easier to

work, and cast-iron plates were nailed over the wood to make it last longer. Often, flanges were put on the rails so that ordinary cartwheels could use the railway too.

The first modern-style iron rails were laid in 1789 by William Jessop in central England. They were made of cast-iron in short lengths of about a metre and broke rather easily. However, the efficiency of the new metal rails was proved by the Surrey Iron Railway, probably the world's first public freight railway. In its opening test of 1803, a single horse hauled a 55-tonne load and 50 people.

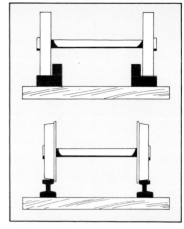

Above: Flanges to guide the wheels were first put on the rails (top) then on the wheels themselves (bottom).

Below: Wooden rails have been used since the 16th century to guide horse-drawn wagons.

The Spread of the Railways

In 1830, the world's first entirely steam-hauled passenger railway opened, linking Manchester and Liverpool in the north of England. It ran to a timetable, had proper stations and **signals**, and carried fare-paying passengers as well as freight. The age of railways had begun.

During the 1830s, countries all over the world began to build railways. Better locomotive and rail design allowed faster running times and fewer breakdowns. Engines became larger, with extra **axles** to support their weight. As longer journeys became possible, larger **tenders** were needed to carry enough coal and water.

At first, British locomotives and designs were exported to other countries. For example, in 1829 the English-built *Stourbridge Lion* was the first locomotive to run on a public track in the United States. Also, the first German public railway was opened by *Der Adler*, a locomotive built by Robert Stephenson's Company.

The export of British locomotives meant that the British standard **gauge** (width of track) of 4ft 8½ins (1.43 metres) became widespread throughout Europe. However, Spain and Russia adopted wider gauges, and travellers must still change trains at national borders where different gauges meet.

By 1844 there were over 3540 kilometres of working railway in Britain, and by 1850 the rail network linked all its major towns. Elsewhere the process took longer, partly because of greater distances and partly because of a later start. By 1870 most European countries had extensive networks.

However there were no railways yet in China, Japan or most of Africa. Four Australian states and New Zealand were just entering the railway age. The great railway systems of South America were only just beginning to expand. The USA had only one-fifth of its present network and Canada only one-twentieth.

Above: The Liverpool and Manchester Railway opened on 15 September 1830. It used steam engines on all its trains and was the world's first modern railway.

Below: The first German public railway was opened in 1835 between Nuremburg and Furth. *Der Adler* hauled its first train.

Great Races to the North

In countries like Britain and America, private companies competed for passengers, often over the same routes. This led to wasteful doubling-up of tracks, but it also speeded up the building of rail networks.

Intense rivalry also led to faster running. In Britain, for example, two companies jointly worked the west coast route from London to Edinburgh via Crewe, which in 1887 was scheduled to take 10 hours. Three other companies combined to operate the east coast route via York. The fastest east coast service, the *Flying Scotsman*, took only 9 hours. In June 1888, the west coast speeded up their service by a full hour. The east coast promptly cut their journey time to $8\frac{1}{2}$ hours. The west coast announced that they would match this, but on the same day, the east coast cut another 30 minutes!

The very next day, the west coast announced it would match the new 8-hour record. The eyes of the world were on the *Caledonian 123*.

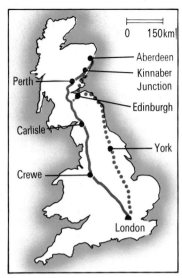

Above: The west coast route via Crewe, and the east coast via York.

Above: In 1888, the unique *Caledonian 123* hauled the winning train from Carlisle to Edinburgh.

Her crew rose to the occasion and she surprised everyone by arriving 8 minutes early! Details of her run were telegraphed to newspapers around the world.

Eventually, worried about the costs and risks involved in competing, both sides agreed to stop racing and stick to their schedules. But the uneasy truce was broken in 1895 when racing began on the London to Aberdeen journey. The two routes joined at a place called Kinnaber Junction. Both sides made secret adjustments to their schedule to try to get their train past this junction first.

Public interest in these races was tremendous, and they had a lasting effect on people's expectations of fast rail travel. Indeed the west coast's London-to-Aberdeen record speed of 63.3mph (101 km/h) was not improved on until the late 1970s, by the diesel 125 engines.

Across Continents

During the 19th century, the world's great continents were spanned by railways. Europe, North America, Russia and Australia were each in turn linked from coast to coast by great iron highways.

Australia's first transcontinental railway was completed in 1917. It includes the world's longest straight – 478 kilometres of completely straight track across the arid and treeless Nullarbor Plain.

In Australia, different states began their railways independently, using various locomotives and adopting a mixture of narrow, standard and broad gauges (see page 53). This meant that people and freight had to be transferred from one train to another at state borders. (By 1969, however, the journey from Perth to Sydney of 3960 kilometres could be made on standard gauge.)

In North America, as each railroad track reached into new territory, the company was given land alongside it by the government as a reward. As in Britain, there was fierce rivalry, with up to

By 1917, it was possible to cross Australia using three different gauges.

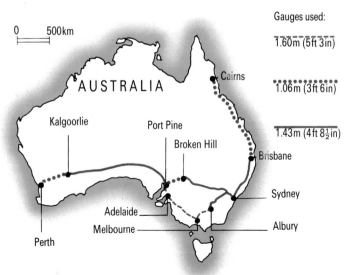

Gauges used:

1.60m (5ft 3in)

1.06m (3ft 6in)

1.43m (4ft 8½in)

three companies competing on some routes. By 1860 over 48,280 kilometres of American railroad was in use.

In May 1869, the link was completed between Chicago and California, a journey of 2776 kilometres crossing difficult territory including the Rocky Mountains. It was the world's first transcontinental railway. Two companies, Union Pacific and Central Pacific, had raced each other at track-laying from opposite directions. The government paid them a grant according to the distance laid.

Canada was not far behind. The Canadian Pacific route from Montreal to Van-

Above: In 1869, the Last Spike ceremony joined the American railroads from the west and east coasts.

couver – a journey of 4636 kilometres – was completed in November 1885. Even today it takes three days to complete the journey.

In Russia, the Trans-Siberian Railway linked Moscow to Vladivostok, making it the world's longest railway at 9338 kilometres. Most of it was built at great speed between 1891 and 1899. Nowadays it includes the world's longest stretch of electrified railway: 5214 kilometres altogether.

A Time of Change

Above: The railways brought great wealth, but railway towns were often noisy, dirty and overcrowded.

The railways soon showed that they were not merely a new form of transport; they changed the whole pattern of people's lives.

In North America, the railways carried millions of settlers westward, opening up the Great Plains and finally destroying the native Indian way of life. In Europe, the industrial revolution depended on the train's ability to move heavy loads quickly and cheaply. New towns grew up at central rail points. In Britain, building engines and **rolling stock** became a major industry and British locomotives were exported all over the world.

The railways had political effects, too. The British built and controlled the Indian railways, and thus tightened their military control of the Indian people. The Russians used their railways to extend their control of central Asia.

Railways created city suburbs by allowing people to commute to work. Life was quieter and more comfortable for those who lived in the suburbs. At the same time, steam trains made the city centres dirtier and noisier, and people moved out.

Railway Time

The arrival of railway timetables led to new attitudes to time and time-keeping. Before the railways, travel was very slow and a day's travel west or east made little difference. People in each place simply set their clocks by the Sun, taking noon to be whenever the Sun was at its highest. No-one worried about the fact that every little town was on its own local time.

Once trains started running to timetables, zones were needed with an agreed time. Small countries had a single time zone, whereas countries like America had several time zones, with the west coast running 3 hours behind the east. Whenever a transcontinental train crossed a time zone, its passengers adjusted their watches.

Below: In America, small towns sprang up along the railroad routes.

The Age of Steam

For about a hundred years, steam trains were very popular. Standards of speed, safety and comfort were rising all the time. Continuing improvements in the design of locomotives, carriages and track meant that more people began to travel over longer distances, for a wider range of purposes.

Meals on Wheels

As carriages became more comfortable, people were encouraged to make longer journeys. At first, long-distance trains made meal stops at certain stations. In the early days of the British races (see page 12) some of the improvements in journey times were made at the expense of the meal stop. Hundreds of passengers being fed a four-course lunch within 20 minutes at Preston during a record-breaking run must have been an amazing sight!

In the 1880s, special restaurant cars containing kitchens were developed to feed passengers while on board. These added to the total load the engine had to pull, but cut out the need for meal stops and so encouraged

Below: An early sleeping car, as shown at the Paris Exhibition of 1868.

passengers to spend more on refreshments.

Overnight Travel

In the 1860s, carriages began to be adapted to help people to sleep on long journeys. In America, a cabinet-maker called George Pullman had the idea of making the daytime seats pull out to meet over the foot space. He also built folding berths into the ceiling. By making up beds at both levels, one coach could accommodate 24 passengers lying flat. Pullman's *Pioneer* of 1865 was the first true sleeping car.

In Europe, sleeping cars tended to have four berths within each compartment, rather than spreading them

Above: Trains encouraged people to travel, both on day trips and holidays abroad.

throughout the coach. This gave greater privacy, but fitted fewer people into the space. Following Pullman's example, European sleeping cars began to be fitted with lavatories, better lighting and more effective heating, too.

In countries with well-developed networks, the railways became an important part of the nation's social life. Railway holidays promoted seaside resorts. Day-trippers and holiday-makers flocked to the coast using scheduled trains and special excursions.

Trains at War

At the time of the American Civil War (1861–1865), the railroads in America depended on small rugged engines, suited to rough tracks and difficult conditions. Because they burned wood, not coal, their range was limited. A full load of wood might last for only 80 kilometres.

The *General* belonged to the Confederacy (southern states), but was hijacked by soldiers from the Union Army (northern states). Their plan was to destroy the Confederates' communications by blowing up a key wooden bridge. Union soldiers disguised as passengers stole the train while its crew were having breakfast. The driver chased after them,

first on a rail handcart, then on a small ironworks engine.

The *General* had a headstart, but kept being delayed by oncoming trains on the

Left: The *General*, the most famous locomotive of the American Civil War.

single-track line. Then the Confederates took over a faster engine called *Texas* and nearly caught up, getting within rifle range. Eventually, after a chase lasting 8 hours, the *General* ran out of fuel, its kidnappers having burned all the carriages in their desperate escape bid.

The World Wars

In World War I (1914–1918), trains were used by both sides to move soldiers, ammunition and supplies to and from the scene of battle. Britain and France built special armour-plated trains to withstand gunfire. The German invasion of Russia was also supported by trains. But because of the broad-gauge Russian track, the Germans had to lay an extra rail before their standard-gauge trains could advance.

During World War II (1939–1945), special locomotives were built to meet the exceptional demands for carrying troops and supplies. The advance of the German army depended on the *Kriegslocomotiv*, a **class** which proved such a strong and reliable design that 8000 of them were built.

Below: The *Kriegslocomotiv*. Survivors of this class are still working in countries like Turkey and Poland.

The 1920s and '30s

Between the Wars, progress in speed and comfort continued. Locomotives were built with bigger boilers for more power, needing more wheels to spread the weight. Carriages became more comfortable, with better seats and more facilities. Sometimes a set of coaches was matched to a particular engine, with the whole train painted in a special design or **livery**.

In 1935, the London and North Eastern Railway (LNER) introduced its *Silver Jubilee* service, a silver-painted matching set of engine and five carriages. Some of these prestige trains were also streamlined. The smooth shape at both ends was supposed to help the train to slide through the air at high speed.

There was fierce competition for the world steam speed record at this time. In 1935, a German engine made by Borsig was the first to travel at 200 km/h. Three years later, the *Mallard* (an LNER engine designed by Nigel Gresley) beat this with a new world record of 203 km/h.

In America, streamlined express trains in special

Above: The *Mallard* is the world steam speed record-holder. It is preserved in running order at York, in England.

Right: The *Chapelon 4–8–4*, perhaps the finest steam engine ever built. It was powerful, fast and very economical.

liveries were also popular. The service between San Francisco and Los Angeles was called *Daylight Express* after its bright daylight colours and because it completed its journey in daylight. It took under 10 hours to travel the 756-kilometre journey.

The fastest of all the scheduled steam services was the *Hiawatha* in the midwest (see page 72).

The New York Central Railroad had a tradition of

fast running on its *Empire State* service between New York and Chicago. In 1893, their famous No. 999 express had claimed to be the first to travel at more than 100mph (160 km/h). By 1943, their scheduled time for covering the 1493 kilometres was only 16 hours – nearly 4 hours faster than it is today!

Meanwhile in France, André Chapelon, one of the finest steam engineers of all time, designed a series of superb engines. His passenger expresses set new standards of speed, economy and reliability for the Paris-Orleans line. His later designs included one of the finest steam engines ever built, known as the 4–8–4 after its **wheel arrangement** (see page 45). It was as powerful as the giant American locomotives nearly twice its size, yet it was one of the most economical engines to run, using only two-thirds of the coal and water that *Mallard* needed.

Giants of Steam

The final flowering of steam engine design was during the 1940s and '50s. This was the age of the biggest and most powerful steam engines of all time, especially in America.

In 1941, the Union Pacific Railway introduced *Big Boys* – massive engines with two sets of **driving wheels** which were **articulated** (able to swivel around corners – see pages 46–47). They were designed for pulling long freight trains over the Rocky Mountains and hauled loads of over 6000 tonnes.

They burned coal so fast (up to 20 tonnes per hour) that human firemen could not keep up, and they had mechanical stokers. Over 40 metres long and weighing almost 540 tonnes, *Big Boys* were amongst the biggest locomotives ever to be built. Six of the 25 that were built have been preserved.

The Union Pacific could also claim the largest passenger engines. Similar in design to the *Big Boys*, the *Challengers* were among the very few articulated engines built for speed as well as pulling power. A surviving *Challenger* is now the biggest working steam engine in the world.

The Pennsylvania Railroad handled many heavy freight trains at high speed, especially to and from the coal mines. At a time when other railways were beginning to abandon steam power, the Pennsylvania decided to prove its superiority. It built a series of **duplex engines** – engines with two

sets of driving wheels like the *Big Boys*, but unlike them, not articulated. These amazing engines were designed to pull 1000-tonne coal trains at up to 160 km/h, and there are reports that they exceeded 192 km/h.

Above: A 1940s Pennsylvania 4–4–4–4 duplex. The unusual streamlining was known as 'shark-nosed'.

Below: *Big Boys* were built for high-speed heavy freight work.

The Challenge to Steam

Since the decline of steam, these engines have become surrounded by romance and nostalgia. Amateur enthusiasts have lovingly restored and redecorated steam trains and operate them as brightly polished tourist attractions.

For the crews who worked the engines, however, the reality was very different. Conditions were often terrible, with a combination of heat, dirt and noise and a total lack of comfort, sometimes not even a seat. In most cases, the **cabs** were open to wind, rain and snow.

Steam trains had other disadvantages, too. They could be inefficient, using a lot of fuel and needing a long time to get up steam before they could do any useful work. The sooty smuts and air pollution produced by burning coal also caused problems, especially in stations and tunnels.

Diesel and Electric

The Baltimore and Ohio Railroad in America introduced the first mainline electric engines in 1895. They pulled trains through the 2-kilometre tunnel out of a Baltimore station. By 1900, electric trains and trams had appeared in several countries. The tramways (street railways) soon gave stiff competition to suburban steam services.

Left: The first mainline electric engine ran on the Baltimore and Ohio Railroad.

The first **diesel** locomotive was built in Britain in 1896, but the first one in public service ran in Sweden in 1913. In the 1920s, a number of American railroads experimented with diesels. By 1940 less than one per cent of all locos in the USA were diesel-powered. Within 25 years, however, diesels had almost entirely taken over.

The choice between diesel or electric engines is finely balanced. Diesel engines can run on any track, but have to carry their own fuel (diesel oil) with them. Electric engines take their power from overhead wires or from special rails. They don't have to carry fuel, but they can only run on electrified track that is expensive to build.

Steam engine-building continued in various countries into the 1960s. The only country that still builds steam engines today is China. At the Datong works a new steam locomotive is completed every few days.

Below: A magnificent old steam engine is broken up for scrap in India.

Travelling by Train

Railways carry two kinds of rail traffic: goods (freight) and people (passengers). Passenger trains are lighter and travel directly between stations. Goods trains are heavier and slower, and often stop along the way to pick up trucks from major customers like steel works and collieries.

Separate stations for passengers and goods are common in cities, but country stations often deal with both. Easy access by road is essential, so that cars, taxis, mailvans and lorries can pick up and set down. Some stations also have links with ships, others with underground and suburban rail services.

Because passenger trains need different numbers of coaches depending on demand, stations were built with **sidings** for spare carriages near to the platforms. Goods sidings are often some distance away with a separate lorry park.

Nowadays, many trains are assembled as rail-car sets, with an engine at each end and a fixed number of coaches. The driver controls

Below: A typical small station on the coast, with links by road and sea.

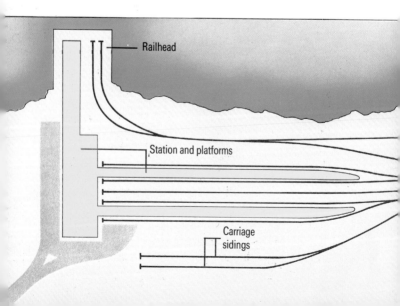

Railhead

Station and platforms

Carriage sidings

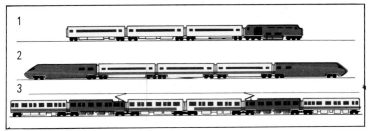

both engines from a cab at either end in push-pull operation.

However, this would be wasteful on commuter trains where most coaches would be empty outside the rush hours. Instead, these trains are made up of one or more self-contained units, according to demand. Typically, each unit might consist of three linked coaches of which the middle one is the **motor-coach**. In a single

1. Engine pulling coaches.
2. Rail-set with two engines linked through coaches.
3. Multiple train, with two units of three coaches.

unit, the driver controls the engine from either end. In a **multiple unit** either of the cabs at the ends of the train controls all the engines. Such trains are called electric multiple units (EMUs) or diesel multiple units (DMUs) depending on their engine.

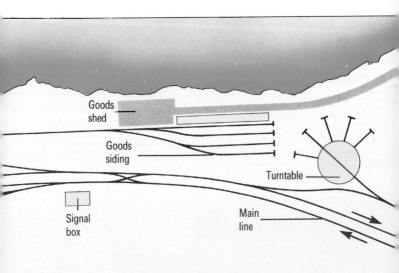

Goods shed

Goods siding

Turntable

Signal box

Main line

Carriages

Above: A Third Class carriage of the Liverpool and Manchester Railway in front of an early First Class carriage of the North Union Railway, with the unusual luxury of oil lighting.

When the first public passenger railways began operating in Britain, there were three classes of passenger accommodation. All were adapted versions of trucks meant for carrying goods. First Class passengers sat in a closed wagon, the Second Class sat in an open wagon, while the Third Class passengers had to stand in an open wagon.

In 1844, an Act of Parliament made a breakthrough for low-cost rail travel. It made all British railways provide at least two trains a day with covered wagons for Third Class passengers at a fare of one (old) penny per mile (£0.004 per 1.60 kilometres). Gradually,

all three classes of accommodation were made more comfortable, as the public came to expect heating, lighting and padded seats.

In most countries nowadays there are basically two classes, though sometimes extra comfort is available by paying extra money. On many Indian trains, for example, passengers in both classes have the option of air conditioning, in fact creating four classes altogether

Easy Access

At first each compartment was quite separate and could only be entered by a door opening onto the platform, though compartments of each class were sometimes

Above: In Pakistan, trains are sometimes so crowded that passengers ride outside the carriages, on the roof and clinging to the sides.

combined in a single coach. Later, corridors were built to allow passengers to move around the train. This allowed access to lavatories, and also to the restaurant cars, observation cars and other special types of carriage which had become a part of rail travel. In addition, corridors allowed ticket collectors and refreshment trolleys to move through the train.

Most carriages now have open seating throughout. In fact, some modern trains are

31

modelled to look like the inside of aircraft – with which they are competing for passengers.

Special Carriages

Passenger trains often carry certain kinds of 'goods' as well as people – for example, newspapers, letters and parcels. The first travelling post offices – special mail-vans attached to fast passenger trains – began to appear in 1838.

These TPO's, as they were called, were specially equipped inside so that people could sort mail during the journey. Outside, nets were fixed to the side of the van to

Above: In front, a travelling post office with nets for non-stop mail handling. Behind, a Canadian Pacific observation car.

allow the train to pick up mail bags from the trackside without stopping. At the same time, bags of sorted mail were dropped for local postmen to deliver within their area.

TPOs gradually died out, partly because of mail robberies and partly because of the rise of large central sorting offices. But a high proportion of the world's mail is still transported by train.

As another means of encouraging people to use the trains, some railway companies which ran along scenic routes began to include observation cars – coaches with extra windows at the sides and sometimes on top as well. You can still travel in observation cars in some countries. One of the finest examples is the Canadian Pacific route from Montreal to Vancouver.

Palaces on Wheels

Queen Victoria was a regular train traveller and had definite ideas about her royal compartments. She offered the London and North Western Railway (LNWR) £800 towards the cost of building two carriages especially for her and her servants and companions, and chose the lavish furnishings personally.

This first 'palace on wheels' set new standards in design. It had sound insulation below the floorboards and a flexible gangway linking the two coaches. The Queen apparently never trusted the link and insisted on stopping the train before crossing from her day saloon to the bedroom!

Below: Part of Queen Victoria's favourite carriage, furnished exactly as she last used it in 1900.

Freight Trucks

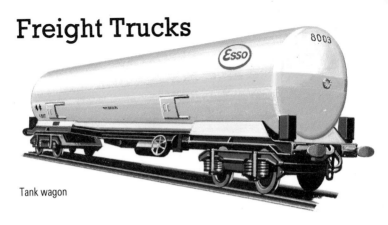

Tank wagon

Railways owe their existence to freight. A single engine can haul a load equivalent to a ship's cargo at great speed, with a total crew of perhaps only two people. This makes rail freight economical for long-range and heavy loads.

Different kinds of trucks are constructed to carry particular loads. Tank wagons are used for carrying oil, petrol and chemicals in loads of 80-100 tonnes. Most tank wagons are owned by the company that fills and empties them. Coal is often carried from collieries to power stations in hopper wagons that can tip over and empty their loads while on the move. This system is sometimes called a 'merry-go-round'.

General goods vans are used for smaller or more varied loads. Wide doors slide along the side to make loading and unloading easier. Customers who want door-to-door transport can pack their goods in standard-sized boxes called containers. These are sealed by the customer, who can feel secure that the contents will not be disturbed. The railway has the advantage that all its container freight can be handled in a standard way. The same container can be transported to its destination anywhere in the world by a combination of rail, road sea and air.

Freight Control

Trucks are sorted out and made up into trains in **marshalling yards**. Incoming trains are pushed over a hump that automatically uncouples each truck. As the truck runs down the hill, the

Hopper wagon   General goods van

control tower changes the points to direct it into the proper siding according to its destination. Metal **retarders** on the tracks make the trucks slow down so that they don't damage each other. Once a train is assembled, it can be shunted back onto the main line.

Below: A marshalling yard:
1. Hump where trucks are uncoupled.
2. Control tower for changing points.
3. Retarders for slowing down trucks.
4. Wagons formed into trains.
5. Lights for marshalling at night.

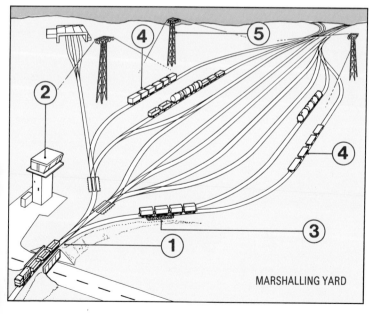

MARSHALLING YARD

Signals and Points

Signals are vital to the safe running of a railway. Because metal wheels slide so smoothly over metal track, no train can brake suddenly. High speed trains carrying large loads may need advance warning of over 3 kilometres before they can stop safely.

The principle of train safety is to divide the track up into suitable blocks, allowing for the longest stopping distance of any train and for the position of any track junctions and stations. No two trains are allowed to travel in the same block of track, and trains cannot go at full speed unless the next few blocks are all clear.

To begin with, signals were given by a man waving coloured flags by the side of the track. Later, mechanical signals imitated the man's

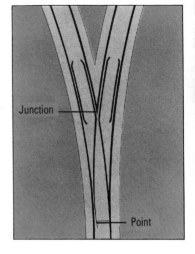

Above: This point is set to direct the train to the left-hand track at the junction.

Below: The track is divided into blocks. Before the train enters each block, the signal warns the driver in advance when to slow down or stop.

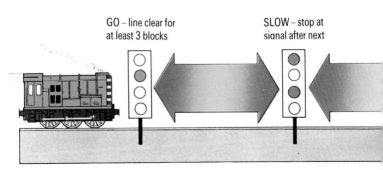

GO – line clear for at least 3 blocks

SLOW – stop at signal after next

arm positions. When the arm was level, the train had to stop. Sometimes there were two arms, one red (the home or immediate signal) and one yellow (the distant or advance warning signal). Later, coloured lights were added to these arms for visibility at night. Most modern signals consist of electric lights. The number of lights and their position varies, but the meaning of the colours is shown below.

Track junctions are controlled by **points**. Moving the point changes the direction

Above: Inside a modern signal box, points, signals and train positions are shown in lights on a track diagram.

that the train will follow. At first, points were changed by hand, then by cables linked to long levers in a signal-box overlooking the junction.

Later, points were controlled electrically, and the signal-box no longer had to be so close to the junction. Modern signal-boxes often control very long sections of track.

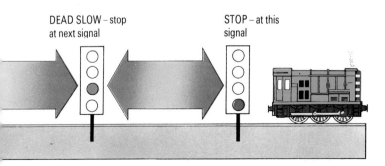

DEAD SLOW – stop at next signal

STOP – at this signal

Safety on the Rails

The first person to be killed on a public railway was a member of the British Parliament. On the opening day of the Liverpool and Manchester Railway in 1830, William Huskisson was run down by *Rocket*. Although he was taken to hospital by the locomotive *Northumbrian*, at a world speed record of 58 km/h, he died of his injuries.

As the speed and volume of railway traffic increased, the need for proper safety measures became more obvious. The block system, described

on page 36, was introduced, with signalmen passing messages up and down the line to each other by telegraph.

Improvements in braking also began to reduce the very long stopping distances. On early trains, brakes were feeble, and could take up to one kilometre to stop a train travelling at 50km/h. At first, the only brakes were on the tender and sometimes in the last coach (the 'brake'

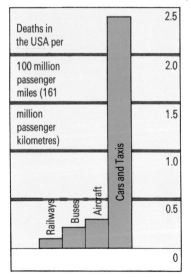

Left: Travelling by train is very safe compared with other forms of transport.

van). If a coupling broke in the middle of a train, runaway coaches and trucks could cause accidents.

The world's worst rail disaster was in France in 1917. A heavily overloaded troop train with only feeble hand-brakes in some coaches was ordered through a steep Alpine tunnel. During the 16-kilometre descent, the brakes became red-hot, set fire to the coaches and the engine derailed, finally wrecking the whole train.

Overall, trains are very safe compared with other

Above: The scattered carriages of a high-speed express train after a fatal accident.

forms of transport. In America, for example, on average in recent years there has been only one death per 1000 million miles (1610 million kilometres). Whereas the rate for internal air traffic is three times greater and for cars and taxis 24 times greater. In some countries there have been recent years when there were no deaths by rail at all.

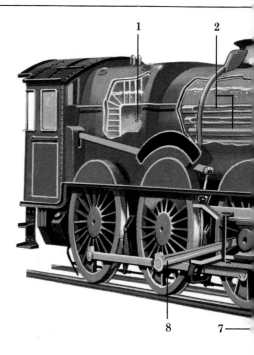

1. Firebox
2. Fire tubes
3. Boiler
4. Chimney
5. Blastpipe
6. Cylinder
7. Piston
8. Connecting rod

Railway Engineering

Some parts of a steam engine are for producing the steam, others are for making the steam turn the driving wheels. Steam is made in the boiler – a large metal barrel containing water. Fuel (coal, wood, or oil) is burned in the firebox. Fire tubes carry the hot air forward from the firebox through the mass of water in the boiler, heating it to boiling-point. Steam forms above the water, and since it cannot escape, the pressure builds up.

The cylinders and wheels turn this steam into useful work. When the pressure is high enough, the driver opens the regulator valve to let steam into the cylinders.

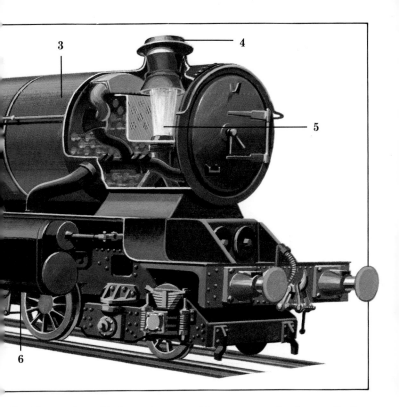

3

4

5

6

Inside each cylinder, steam pressure pushes a piston to the other end of the cylinder. Then steam is let into the other end of the cylinder, forcing the piston back again. Cylinder valves control the intake of steam and also maintain the pressure by stopping any steam from escaping.

This back-and-forth motion of the piston turns the engine wheels through a system of connecting rods, in the same sort of way that a cyclist's up-and-down pressure on the pedals makes a bicycle wheel rotate.

After each stroke of the piston, exhaust steam is forced up the blastpipe and out through the chimney. This sucks the hot gases from the firebox along the fire tubes, making the fire burn steadily. The rush of steam up the blastpipe is what makes each 'puff' from a steam train.

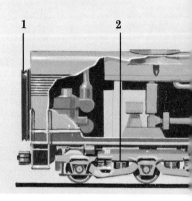

Diesel Engines

Heavy diesel oil is stored in the fuel tank. It is fed to the diesel engine where it is burned under pressure inside a cylinder. This causes a controlled explosion which forces the piston outward. The piston makes a metal rod called a crankshaft rotate. To keep the crankshaft turning regularly the engine may have anything from four to sixteen cylinders.

In a **diesel-electric** engine, the crankshaft drives big **generators** that make electricity. This drives the motors that turn the wheels. **Diesel-mechanical** engines transmit the power to the wheels through a gearbox.

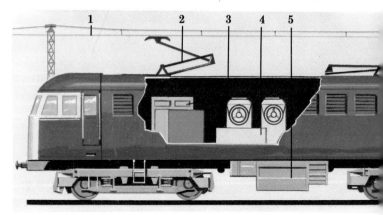

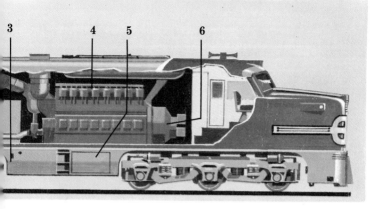

Electric Engines

Electric engines pick up power either from a 'live' third rail on the track, or from overhead wires. This high-voltage electricity has to be stepped down by a **transformer** to a lower voltage. **Rectifiers** then turn it into the steady direct current needed by the electric motors that drive the train. Rectifiers get very hot, and must be cooled by blowers.

An electric train works in much the same way as a diesel-electric. The main difference is that the diesel-electric burns its own fuel to generate electricity, whereas the electric train picks up the current from outside.

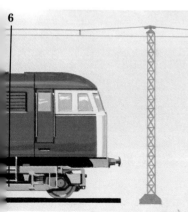

British Rail Class 85 Electric:
1. Overhead wires carrying electric current
2. Pantograph to collect current
3. Rectifier
4. Transformer
5. Emergency batteries
6. Electric motor

Climbing Hills

The great ability of a train to pull heavy loads on the level relies on the smooth slip of steel wheel over steel rail. This slippiness makes it hard for trains to climb hills, when good **adhesion** is essential.

Some early trains used to carry buckets of sand to sprinkle on the rails to improve their grip. Later, many trains had automatic sanding devices.

The steeper the **gradient**, the greater the problem of adhesion. Engines designed for hilly tracks need to have

Right: A gradient of 1 in 10 means one unit up for every ten units *along* the slope.

their weight concentrated over the driving wheels. On the other hand, too much weight on a single axle could damage the track. So powerful engines have their weight spread over many driving wheels. Other wheels, known as leading and trailing

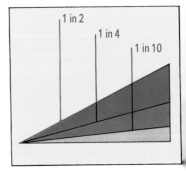

Left: Double-heading a heavy freight train in Africa.

One way of increasing hill-climbing ability is to add a second engine. When two steam engines haul a train, it is called a **double-header** (both engines in front). Many diesel and electric rail sets have one engine at each end.

If a route has only a few steep hills, engines may get help just for the hilly sections. A **banking engine** joins the train at the bottom of a hill, helps to push from the back and then drops off at the summit. The banking engine stays behind in order to help the next train.

wheels may be added in front of and behind the driving wheels to spread the weight further. Different engines had different combinations of wheels, depending on their use. Today, engines are often described in terms of their wheel arrangements.

The heavier the train, the greater the power the engine needs to climb a given hill.

Below: Various wheel arrangements. The figures show the total number (i.e. counting two wheels for each axle) of leading, driving and trailing wheels respectively.

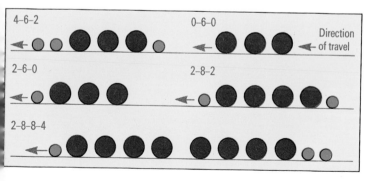

45

Rounding Bends

In general, the shorter the locomotive, the tighter the curve it can follow. However, the most obvious way to increase an engine's power also means increasing its overall length. By 1900, powerful steam engines tended to have long, heavy boilers, whose weight had to be spread over many axles. But if all the wheels had been fixed, the train would only have been able to travel on the straightest of tracks.

Carriages had overcome the length problem early on, by having two sets of wheels

Above: Garratt's double-engine design allows a powerful locomotive to round tight bends.

mounted on **bogies** – swivelling trolleys positioned under the base of the carriage – instead of being fixed to the carriage itself. Bogies were also sometimes used for leading and trailing wheels on locomotives. This method could be combined with up to about ten fixed driving-wheels, giving plenty of power with reasonable curve-hugging.

As requirements for speed, hill-climbing and loads continued to increase, the search for more power continued. A Russian engine was built with a 4–14–4 wheel arrangement. Unfortunately, it kept coming off the track and causing damage.

One solution was patented by a Swiss called Anatole Mallet in 1884. He mounted a second engine on a pivoted truck at the front, allowing the main body of the locomotive to overhang on tight curves. Unlike most other articulated types, Mallet engines could be used with normal tenders. The design proved reliable, allowing *Big Boys* and other Mallets to haul massive loads over hilly routes.

A quite different approach was patented by an Englishman called Herbert Garratt in 1907. His idea was to link two engines by slinging a boiler between them. The front engine carried the main water tank, while the back one had a lesser water tank and the fuel supply. The boiler supplied steam to both engines, and its weight increased adhesion over the driving wheels.

Below: Two ways to articulate an engine, combining pulling power with curve-hugging.

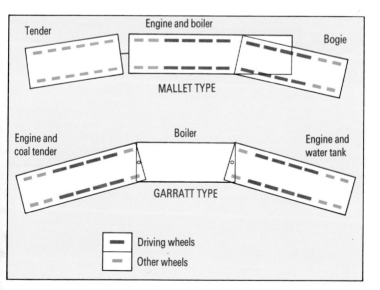

Tender   Engine and boiler   Bogie

MALLET TYPE

Engine and coal tender   Boiler   Engine and water tank

GARRATT TYPE

▬▬▬ Driving wheels
▭▭▭ Other wheels

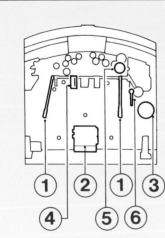

Main controls and gauges:
1. Left and right-hand regulator (throttle), controls the supply of steam and acts as the accelerator.
2. Firebox door for stoking fire.
3. Reversing screw, controls the release of steam and can make train go backwards.
4. Water-level gauge.
5. Steam pressure gauge.
6. Air brake control ('dead man's handle').

How to Drive a Train

Running a steam train involves a lot of preparation and follow-up – greasing all the moving parts, raking out the smokebox, topping up the water, fuel and oil, and so on. The actual driving can be thought of in two stages: getting up steam and then making the train go.

First the fire must be lit and a large tank of water heated from stone-cold to boiling point. Once steam begins to form, the pressure is watched until it is high enough to work the blower. This sends a blast of steam up the chimney and sucks air along the fire tubes, making the fire burn faster and hotter. A higher steam pressure is needed to drive the engine, usually in the range of 10.5 to 21 kg per square centimetre. The whole process of getting up steam takes at least an hour.

Before the train can move off, the cylinders must be heated up. Opening the regulator lets steam into the cold cylinders, but at first it condenses into water. The driver opens the drain cocks (which act like a bath plug) and lets the water and steam gush out of the cylinders.

With the drain cocks shut again, steam pressure builds up ready for the train to go.

The driver controls the speed by opening and closing the regulator. Once the train is cruising along, he uses the reversing screw to shorten the puffs of steam into the cylinders, so as to avoid wasting steam. If the engine is stopped, turning the same control further makes the train move backwards.

All the time the driver must keep stoking the fire and checking the steam pressure and water-level gauges. Steam engines use large amounts of water: *Big Boys* could use up to 50 tonnes per hour! Whenever the water level gets low, the driver must work the injectors. These use steam to heat and inject water from the tank into the boiler.

Stopping the train demands skill and judgement, because the driver must think well in advance and avoid locking the wheels or bumping the different carriages of the train together. The more modern steam trains have air brakes that work on the whole train as well as on the engine.

Electric and Diesel Trains

Electric and diesel loco-
motives are much easier to
drive than steam engines. No
warming-up time is needed
before the train can move
and there are fewer routine
jobs to do between each run.
The controls are simpler and
more uniform. The cab is
quieter and much more comfortable, with a large wind-
screen with wipers to give
the driver a clear view.
Coloured indicator lights
glow to warn the driver of
any faults – for example if the
wheels are slipping. In bad
weather, a wall-mounted
warning system containing

coloured discs automatically
changes colour to match that
of the track signal ahead.

However, driving any kind
of train is still a skilled job
because the driver is respon-
sible for the safety of the
passengers. Many of the
driver's controls and duties
are concerned with safety.
For example, unless the
driver presses a foot-pedal all
the time the brakes will come
on automatically. The pur-
pose of this pedal (sometimes
called a 'dead man's handle')
is to prevent an accident if
the driver is taken ill or falls
asleep. There is a speedometer to help him observe the

Main controls in an electric cab:
1. Automatic warning system.
2. Main train brake with locomotive brake behind it.
3. Speedometer dial.
4. Main controller – acts as the accelerator.
5. Forward/reverse handle.
6. Driver's safety device.

speed limits for junctions and bends.

To start an electric train, the driver turns a master key, puts the forward/reverse handle in the correct position and feeds power to the motors using the main controller. This must be done gradually to make the train move away smoothly, without wheelspin. If the train collects its current through a **pantograph** on the roof, the driver may first have to press the button that lifts it up to the power wires.

Driving a diesel-electric train is very similar. There are no pantograph controls, but the driver must ensure he has enough diesel oil for the journey. He starts the diesel engine by pressing a button, and must keep an eye on its performance with the help of various dials and lights.

Diesel-mechanical locomotives are controlled slightly differently. The driver uses a gearbox to match the torque (turning power) of the engine to the conditions, just like driving a lorry. Getting started and climbing hills both need a lot of torque and a low gear. Once the train is under way, less torque is needed and a higher gear lets the train move faster.

Designing a Railway Route

Designing the layout of a railway track is not as straightforward as it might seem. The shortest route between two places is not necessarily the easiest for a train. Trains cannot climb very steep hills and need much longer, flatter routes than cars, for example. **Cuttings** and **embankments** have to be built to keep a railway route level in places where a road would simply dip down and back up again.

The layout of every route is governed by a ruling gradient – the steepest slope which is allowable. A ruling gradient of 1 in 30 is considered steep, and 1 in 50 more normal.

A steep ascent can be made more gradual by spreading it over a greater length of track, for example using wide S-bends or even spiral track. The curves cannot be too tight, however, or large locomotives would not be able to get round them (see page 46). So although tunnels are expensive to build, they are sometimes a better solution because they make the route more direct and flatter. Railways across the Alps depend on tunnels, the longest being the Simplon Tunnel at 21.6 kilometres.

Left: The shortest route is not always the best; tunnels and viaducts look impressive but are expensive to build.

Sometimes the only solution is to combine a spiral route with tunnelling in the mountain. On the Canadian Pacific route through the Rocky Mountains, there are two spiral tunnels in Kicking Horse Pass.

Tunnels also allow railways to go under the sea. The Seikan Tunnel of the Japanese Shinkansen Railway, due to open in 1986, will be the world's longest tunnel at 53.8 kilometres, linking Hokkaido island with mainland Japan.

Using broad-gauge rail increases the costs of track-laying, tunnelling and other engineering works. However, it also allows the carriages to be wider and more comfortable and to hold more people. Narrow-gauge railways are cheaper to build, but they suffer from the problem of interchange with standard-gauge track.

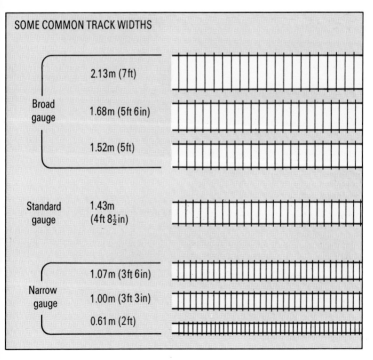

SOME COMMON TRACK WIDTHS

Broad gauge
- 2.13m (7ft)
- 1.68m (5ft 6in)
- 1.52m (5ft)

Standard gauge
- 1.43m (4ft 8½in)

Narrow gauge
- 1.07m (3ft 6in)
- 1.00m (3ft 3in)
- 0.61m (2ft)

Building a Railway

Railway building was a major industry in the 19th century. Cuttings were dug and embankments were built up by labourers, using brute strength and simple tools like picks and shovels. These gangs of navvies, as they were called, had no modern machines or explosives to help them. Yet many of their railway routes still stand as great feats of engineering.

Huge teams of navvies were sent around the country, moving on after completing each stretch of

track. They often slept in tents or wooden huts set up near the route. Respectable people feared them and thought of them as unruly mobs.

Below: Track-laying by hand on the Union Pacific in the 1860s.

Sleeper   Rail

The navvies have gone, but in spite of modern machinery, basic methods of railway-building have changed very little. Once a route has been decided, there are two main jobs: preparing the track-bed and laying the rails. The ground is smoothed out and packed down to make a firm base. Wooden **sleepers** are laid at right angles to the direction of travel to support the rails. The rails are fixed to the sleepers with bits of metal of various shapes, called spikes, clips or chairs. The track and sleepers are weighted down by ballast (small stones) over the track bed.

Above: Working round the clock to keep high-speed trains running in Japan. Inset: Cross-section through a modern high-speed rail.

Rails used to be laid in lengths of around 20 metres, with small gaps in between to allow for expansion during hot weather. Today special track-laying vehicles often weld the rails into continuous track before laying it, making the joins very smooth and silent. On high-speed routes, concrete sleepers have replaced straight wooden ones. They give a firmer base and need less ballast and maintenance.

55

Special Railways

An amazing variety of railways exist for special purposes. They have been built underground, up mountains, on the sea bed and in every possible gauge.

Underground Railways

The sudden growth of cities at the end of the last century brought large numbers of workers into their centres, all at the same time. Narrow streets became clogged with horse traffic, and densely-packed buildings made it impossible to find space for surface railways. To reach the city centres, railways had to go underground.

The first underground railway in the world appeared in London. In 1900, the Paris Metro and the New York Subway both opened.

All of these railways were steam-operated at first. The dirt and fumes must have been overpowering, and the driver had no protection – not even a cab. One interesting exception was the Glasgow Underground, which opened in 1896 using a cable system. The trains gripped a cable which was wound continuously around a huge drum by a single stationary steam engine. Its smoke could be kept well away from

Left: Baker Street station in the days when the London underground was steam-operated.

the drivers and passengers.

Many other cities opened underground railways between the two World Wars, using electric power from the start. Madrid opened its system in 1919, Sydney in 1926, Tokyo in 1927 and Moscow in 1933. The Moscow system was perhaps the most ambitious. Its stations have huge chandeliers and murals to proclaim the achievements and successes of the Soviet State.

To begin with, all undergrounds were made by boring tunnels under the built-up land. But tunnel-boring is very expensive and using explosives can be dangerous. Where the surface is less built-up, a shallow underground track can be made by a different method called 'cut-and-cover'. A deep cutting is carved out, and after the track is laid a long continuous bridge is built to roof it over. Then the bridge is covered with earth and the surface is restored.

Below: The Stockholm underground opened in 1950.

Modern Metros

After 1945, planners thought that city transport would depend on private motor cars. In many cities, money was put into building urban motorways. The railway networks were not developed, and in some cities they were neglected and allowed to run down.

By the late 1950s, the costs and effects of private motoring in cities were better understood. New metros began to spring up in cities all over the world. Lisbon and Haifa opened metros in 1959, Kiev in 1960 and Milan in 1964. In 1966, Montreal opened a splendid new metro

Above: Trains at different levels at Lionel-Groulx, a station in the modern metro system in Montreal.

with rubber-tyred wheels for smooth and quiet running.

City Railways

Underground railways vary in their depth below the surface. Some have sections where the track comes above ground. However, most were built as self-contained systems without links to mainline railways, buses or other forms of transport.

The BART (Bay Area Rapid Transit) scheme was developed in the early 1970s

in California. It is a far-reaching system that provides a modern electric rail service to cities throughout the area surrounding San Francisco Bay. It has been carefully planned for easy interchange with other forms of transport, like the new metro and tramways (streetcars). It even helps people who want door-to-door transport by giving free parking to cars and bicycles.

Paris is another city with a well-planned transport system. Its extensive metro is linked with the rapid suburban rail service called the R.E.R. Many stations interchange with both systems, which together form a vast network covering hundreds of kilometres.

Below: Richmond Platform of the Bay Area Rapid Transit (BART) – a fine modern city system.

Industrial Railways

All over the world, special railways have been built for factories, quarries, mines and farms. Some were in action before the mainline passenger services. Simple wagon-ways worked in mines, transporting coal along underground passages long before the steam engine was developed. Even today, most mines have large underground railways, usually worked by diesel or electric engines.

Many mines, factories and docks have private tracks which link up with the public railways, making it easier and cheaper to handle the goods. In Britain, for example, the National Coal Board still has an extensive standard-gauge rail system.

One of the biggest industrial systems in the world today is the Capital Iron and Steel Works at Beijing (Peking) in China. Here, 45 large steam engines transport raw materials and heavy bars of

Below: A British-built train at work in India, pulling an unusual load of dried dung, useful as fuel.

steel around many kilometres of track within the factory itself. Smaller engines are also used in steel works elsewhere, for example in Turkey.

Above: Molten waste from steel being poured onto a slag heap beside an industrial railway in Karabuk, Turkey.

Industrial locomotives are not only found near towns. The narrow-gauge railways of the Welsh mountains were built over a century ago to carry slate from quarries to the coast. Nowadays, they belong to railway enthusiasts, and help to attract tourists from all over the country.

In many countries, industries like farming and forestry are important to the economy. Narrow-gauge railways have been built to serve sugar and tea plantations, lumber yards and farms.

Old steam locomotives often work these lines, some of them purchased long ago from mainline companies at little more than scrap price. On sugar plantations, steam engines sometimes burn bagasse – a waste product from sugar processing which is freely available. Some of the world's oldest working steam engines are still in operation in places like India and the Philippines.

61

Mountain Railways

Smooth metal wheels grip metal track best on the level. However, many mountainous areas depend on railways for basic transport.

Conventional railways can be designed with lots of tunnels and viaducts to reduce steep gradients (see page 52). One Spanish railway has 182 tunnels in only 177 kilometres.

In mountainous parts of India and Peru, where there is no room for bends or spirals, the tracks use a zig-zag pattern to allow trains to climb more steeply. The train reverses its direction between each section of the Z, changing the points as it climbs.

The world's highest standard-gauge railway has 19 such zig-zags. It is the Central Railway of Peru, which climbs 4775 metres over 172 kilometres, to a terminus high in the Andes. Gradients of 1 in 25 are normal, with long stretches of 1 in 20 or even steeper.

Rack and Cable

Although very high, the Central Railway of Peru still uses conventional smooth wheels gripping straight

Above: Changing directions along each section of a zig-zag allows a train to climb a steep hill, changing the points as it does so.

rails. For even steeper slopes, without enough space for track-laying, there are two main alternatives – rack or cable. Rack railways are generally used for longer routes with bends, and cable railways for short straight sections like cliff railways.

Rack (or cog) railways have special toothed wheels on the trains that lock into a straight toothed rack that runs along the track. The teeth stop the train from slipping back, even on slopes as steep as 1 in 2. Rack railways used to be worked by steam engines, but nowadays most of them are powered by electricity.

Rack railways have been built right up to the summits of high mountains like Mount Pilatus in Switzerland. The Pilatus Railway opened in 1889 with steam power, and was electrified in 1937. It is the steepest of all rack railways, with a gradient of 1 in 2. Its station 'platforms' consist of flights of stairs.

Cable railways (funiculars) depend on a moving cable that each train (or cable-car) grips tightly. A motor (usually electric) keeps the whole cable moving all the time. Any cars attached to the cable are pulled along at the same speed. The cable can run along the ground between the rails, but in very mountainous areas, an overhead cable is often slung between tall pylons, doing away with the need for rails altogether. Steep cable systems are often balanced so that the weight of one train coming down the mountain helps to pull the other one up.

Below: The breathtaking Swiss electric funicular from Murren to Allmendhubel, with the Munch and Eiger mountains behind.

Miniature Railways

Most of the world's mainline railways have been built on track with a gauge of at least one metre. However, useful railways can operate on much narrower track.

One of the most spectacular small railways climbs into the foothills of the Himalayas in northern India. The Darjeeling Himalayan Railway uses a 61-cm gauge. It climbs nearly 2400 metres in its 82-kilometre route, using zig-zags and spiral loops to gain height. Most of the traffic on this line is still pulled by antique steam engines, although some diesels are now being brought into use.

The Romney, Hythe and Dymchurch Railway claims to be the smallest public railway in the world. It stretches nearly 21 kilometres along the south coast of England. Its builder actually described it as the biggest model train set in existence. Nevertheless, during World War II it had a real armoured train which formed part of Britain's coastal defences. Nowadays it still carries regular fare-paying passengers.

Many miniature railways are operated for fun. Fairgrounds and pleasure parks offer rides for children (and adults). Usually the steam

Left: The Darjeeling Himalayan Railway in operation.

engines are faithful replicas of famous full-size locomotives. Some are very old, and were built by engineering apprentices in railway workshops as part of their training.

On very small locomotives, not everything can be reproduced at the correct **scale**. Even where steam power is used, oil often replaces coal as fuel. Steam pressure is much lower than on full-size locomotives. The engine cab is usually far too small to accommodate the driver, who instead sits upon the tender. The carriages are usually no more than flat platforms, which passengers can sit on or astride.

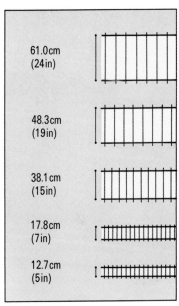

61.0cm (24in)

48.3cm (19in)

38.1cm (15in)

17.8cm (7in)

12.7cm (5in)

Above: Miniature railways are built to very narrow gauges.

Below: A miniature replica of a Great Eastern steam engine.

Model Trains

As long as there have been railway enthusiasts, there have been model railways, designed, built and run for fun. The earliest model trains were all hand built, often with great skill, and ran on specially constructed model track.

In recent years, model trains and ready-made track layouts have been mass-produced and sold through toy-shops. Specialist modelling shops carry an astonishing range of trucks, carriages, signals, station furniture, lighting and people. Anyone with enough money to spend can build up a realistic layout without needing special tools or skill with their hands.

Model trains have been built to a wide range of scales. The diagram shows the main sizes for which a range of ready-made models are sold. The tiny Z gauge has a scale of only 1:220. It allows a complicated layout with lots of junctions, points and stations to be fitted into

Below: The most popular scales for model trains shown actual size. HO and OO share the same gauge.

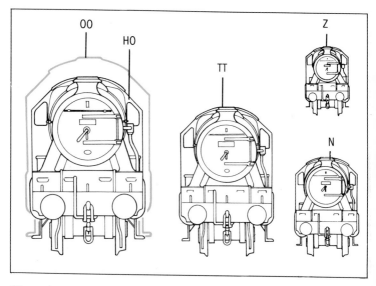

a small space. The N gauge is a little larger (1:160) and TT ('table-top') larger again at a scale of 1:120.

Probably the best-known scales are HO and OO. The OO trains are built to a scale of 4mm to the foot, whereas HO trains are seven-eighths of that size. Both run on track with a gauge of 16.5 mm. The OO scale was invented in Britain, where it is still the most popular one for model trains; it is also found in North America. All OO trains are slightly oversize to allow for the fact that models are often viewed from above. The HO scale is the same (3.5mm to the foot) for both train and track. It is widespread in Europe, the Americas and Australasia.

Most small model trains are run indoors. However, some enthusiasts like to build outdoor railways, perhaps because they have run out of indoor space, or perhaps because of the greater scope offered by garden features like rockeries and pools. Outdoor trains are made of stronger materials so that they can run in any weather. Usually the track is ballasted like its full-size cousin.

Below: Designing and operating model rail layouts is a fascinating hobby for enthusiasts of all ages.

Unusual Trains

Over the years, trains have been built in almost every shape and size imaginable. One of the most amazing was the Listowel and Ballybunion Railway, which opened in Ireland in 1888. It had a single rail supported above the ground by A-shaped trestles. The engine and all the carriages were doubled up and hung over the track like panniers on a donkey.

The system was designed by a Frenchman called Charles Lartigue. It was meant for remote areas where speed did not matter, but cheap track-building was important.

The train included mobile steps so that passengers could climb over the line to keep the balance even. Once, when a piano had to be transported, it was balanced by a cow. To return the cow to its owner, two calves had to be sent along too. Finally the calves were returned, one on either side.

Similar monorails were built in North Africa, central France, Russia, Guatemala and Peru. However, the system was too inflexible and never really caught on.

The Brighton and Rottingdean Seashore Electric Tramroad opened in 1896. Its body was shaped like a ship's cabin, supported on 7-metre stilts. It had an 18-foot (5.5-metre) gauge track which

ran along the seashore. At high tide the track was covered in water. Unfortunately, the rails were too easily damaged by wind and waves and kept needing major repairs. The Tramroad closed in 1901.

Above: Changing the points was a major performance on this amazing Irish railway.

Below: The Brighton Electric Tramroad carried holiday-makers along the seashore in up to 5 metres of water.

Famous Trains

Throughout the history of the railways, there have always been locomotives or services which have stood out for their high standards of speed or luxury.

The Flying Scotsman

In Britain, the same spirit of competition between the East and West coast services that had led to the 'Great Races' (see page 12) continued into the 20th century.

In 1928, in an attempt to outdo the West Coast company, the East Coast introduced a non-stop express service over the whole 632-kilometre route between London and Edinburgh – making it the longest non-stop service in the world. The service was christened the *Flying Scotsman*.

The most powerful class of passenger locomotives used on the East Coast line was the A3 Pacific class, designed by Sir Nigel Gresley, and introduced in 1922. To allow the crew to switch over on the long journey, Gresley designed a special tender for these locomotives with a small corridor enabling the crew to pass between the

engine and the leading carriage. The *Flying Scotsman* locomotive was a member of this class. It was the first British engine to achieve an officially recognized speed of 100mph (160 km/h).

The title *Flying Scotsman* is still given to the fastest London to Edinburgh service today. However, the journey is now completed in $4\frac{1}{2}$ hours by the Inter-City 125s, the fastest diesel locomotives in the world.

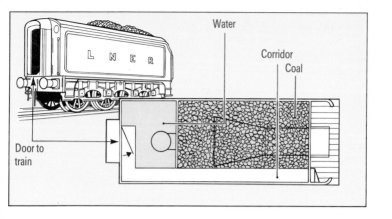

Above: The corridor tender which allowed for a change of crew during the non-stop journey from London to Edinburgh.

Below: Built in 1925, the *Flying Scotsman* has been preserved in running order at Carnforth railway museum in Lancashire.

The Hiawatha

In America during the 1930s, an intense rivalry sprang up on the route between Chicago and the twin cities of Minneapolis/St. Paul. Three companies were involved – the Chicago and North Western, the Chicago, Burlington and Quincy and the Milwaukee Road.

The Burlington route introduced a fast but noisy diesel service. At the same time, the North Western express covered the 656 kilometres in 400 minutes using conventional steam-powered trains. The Milwaukee Road company responded by introducing the fastest of all steam express services, the *Hiawatha*. The engines were designed for a $6\frac{1}{2}$-hour scheduled time over the slightly longer route of 663 kilometres. These were the first locomotives ever designed to operate daily at speeds of over 100mph (160 km/h).

The first batch of *Hiawatha* engines had a 4–4–2 wheel arrangement and at the time they were the biggest and fastest trains in the world. Although designed to pull trains of only six carriages, they regularly

handled nine-carriage trains *and* cut the journey time to just $6\frac{1}{4}$ hours. Larger locomotives were introduced in 1938, with a 4–6–4 wheel pattern. They were intended to pull 12-carriage trains.

The *Hiawatha* service still holds the world record for the fastest-ever, start-to-stop run between two stations on a scheduled route under steam power – it averaged 130km/h over a 127-kilo-

The streamlined locomotives of the Milwaukee Road company operated the fastest steam passenger service in the world over a route between Chicago and Minneapolis/St. Paul.

metre stretch in Wisconsin. The *Hiawatha* also has claims on the world steam speed record. Trains often went at over 193 km/h, but claims that they surpassed *Mallard's* record of 203 km/h (see page 22) have never been confirmed.

At first, the *Hiawatha* was a great commercial success. The service was doubled-up for a time, when the *Morning Hiawatha* also ran on the same line. However, diesel power began to replace steam in 1941, and by the late 1940s, steam had disappeared from this route for ever.

Today, there is a diesel service over the *Hiawatha* route. However, track maintenance has been so poor that the minimum journey time is now over 10 hours – nearly 4 hours slower than the steam trains of fifty years earlier.

Orient Express

Early railway travel tended to be primitive, but by the 1860s, attempts were being made to introduce luxury trains. In America, George Pullman's carriages had changed people's standards of comfort, and Pullman's influence was also felt in Europe. In 1876, the Belgian designer Georges Nagelmackers set up the famous Wagons-Lits Company, which operated comfortable sleeping-car trains across Europe.

Wagons-Lits' first *Orient Express* service began operating in 1833 from Paris to Vienna. Later it was extended through Hungary and Romania to the port of Giurgi, where passengers boarded a boat to Constantinople (now Istanbul). The rail connection to Constantinople was completed in 1889.

The heyday of luxury train travel was between the World Wars. The name *Orient Express* became attached to a network of services, the most famous being the Venice-Simplon-Orient Express. Linked to a boat-train service from London, it ran from Paris to Istanbul via Milan and Venice, crossing

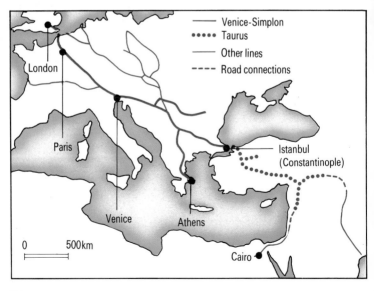

- ——— Venice-Simplon
- ••••• Taurus
- ——— Other lines
- - - - Road connections

London

Paris

Venice

Athens

Istanbul (Constantinople)

0   500km

Cairo

Above: The restored *Orient Express* recreates the period feel of the 1920s. Inset: Elegant wining and dining in the restaurant car.

the Alps through the Simplon Tunnel.

The Arlberg-Orient Express ran through southern Germany and Austria, connecting with the Simplon Express at Belgrade. Other trains from Berlin and Prague linked with the Arlberg at Vienna and Budapest. The Taurus Express carried passengers onward from Istanbul through Turkey to Damascus. Links to Baghdad and Cairo were never completed.

Wartime ended the luxury services by 1940. Although attempts were made to revive them after 1945, by then the Iron Curtain had divided Europe and the *Orient Express* name sometimes meant no more than one sleeping car linked to a local train. The last left Paris in 1977.

The *Orient Express* service resumed in 1982, with as much luxury as the original. Passengers travel from London to Venice, following the old route exactly.

TGV

TGV stands for *Train à Grande Vitesse* – French for 'high-speed train'. Plans for a new electric high-speed train were announced by SNCF, the French national railway company, in 1966. The first two experimental trains were tested in 1978, quickly reached their design speed of 260 km/h and even clocked up 314 km/h with no problem.

The TGV is made up of an unvarying set of two locomotives and eight coaches. Four coaches are First Class, seating 135 passengers each, and the rest are Second Class with 240 seats each. Lightweight modern materials and design mean that the whole train weighs only 380 tonnes. The TGV's powerful electric motors give it a high ratio of power to weight, allowing high speeds to be maintained even on steep gradients. Its low centre of gravity permits the train to hug tight curves without tipping over.

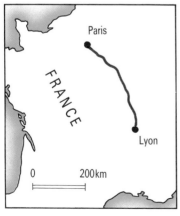

The TGV in action (left), while passengers enjoy First Class meals and comfort (above).

These features were important in the planning of the new TGV high-speed track between Paris and Lyon. The engineers had unusual freedom over both gradients and curves. The line includes hills as steep as 1 in 28.5 (the usual motorway limit is 1 in 25) and its curves are almost as sharp as a motorway's. This allowed the engineers to avoid major earthworks, and so keep track-building costs low. For example, there is not a single tunnel on the line. Further economies were possible in places where new stretches of motorway could actually be built alongside the railway line.

The 425-kilometre line was completed in 1983, when an incredible journey time of exactly 2 hours became the normal schedule for 60 trains a day. Thundering along at an *average* speed of 212 km/h, the TGV not only brings Lyon closer to Paris, it also shrinks the rail map of Europe. For example, Geneva, previously $5\frac{3}{4}$ hours from Paris by the fastest train, is now only $3\frac{1}{4}$ hours away. This compares well with the time by air, when travelling from city centre to city centre.

Safe high-speed running depends on advanced signalling methods (page 86) and on powerful brakes. The TGV's three separate braking systems are controlled automatically. Between them, they can bring a fully loaded train to a dead stop from 260 km/h in just 3.5 kilometres.

The Bullet Train

The *Bullet Trains* run on the Shinkansen lines in Japan, and their performance has set new standards for modern public transport. They carry around 450,000 people per day between Tokyo and all the main cities of Honshu, the mainland of Japan.

The first Shinkansen line opened between Tokyo and Osaka in 1964, only seven years after the project was seriously discussed. This 515-kilometre section, known as the Tokaido Shinkansen, is now one of the world's busiest routes. Over 100 trains a day run in each direction, thundering along at 210km/h, sometimes as little as 4 minutes behind the next train.

Owing to their speed and efficiency, *Bullet Trains* are widely used by Japan's businessmen.

Unlike the TGV, the Shinkansen lines were made as level and as straight as possible. Because land is scarce and costly in Japan, long sections of track were built on low concrete viaducts, and tunnels are frequent (up to 57 per cent of the track on one of the lines).

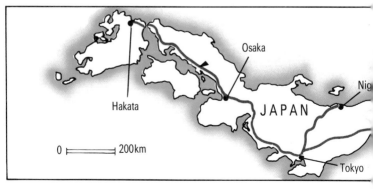

There are no level crossings, no gradients steeper than 1 in 50, and no bends with a radius of less than 2.5 kilometres. The later Shinkansen lines are even flatter and straighter than the original Tokaido line.

Bullet Train passengers have more space and comfort

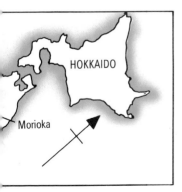

than Japan's old narrow-gauge track allowed. Some cars have wide corridors for wheelchair access, and there are public pay-phones for passengers' use. Trains draw up exactly opposite metal plates on the platforms, labelled with coach and door numbers, so passengers step onto the train at exactly the right place for their seats.

The *Bullet Train* service has cut journey times drastically and has maintained a splendid safety record, with neither death nor injury to any passenger in 20 years. It became profitable within two years of its opening, and by 1980 was contributing one-third of the revenue brought in by all Japanese railways.

The Future

Opinions differ about the future of railways. Some people believe that steady improvements in locomotive and track design will combine to improve speed, reliability and comfort. Others think it more important to improve the links between different forms of mainline and city railways and metros. Others again think that completely new kinds of engines and track will be needed.

Monorails

Many experiments have been made with single-railed track of various kinds. Most,

like the Listowel and Ballybunion (see page 68), were a failure. However, the amazing electric 'hanging train' in Wuppertal, Germany, is a unique example of a working monorail with a long history of success. Kaiser Wilhelm II was among the first 10,000 passengers carried in its first 10 hours of running in 1901.

Nowadays the monorail carries around 50,000 passengers daily, and forms an integral part of the city's public transport system. For 10 of its 13-kilometre length, the track is suspended over the river (above), giving

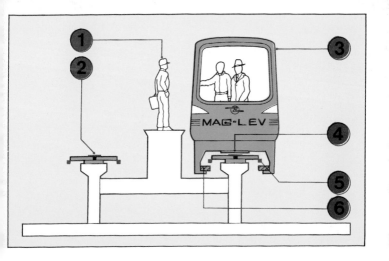

Above: The maglev system:
1. Passenger on raised platform.
2. Aluminium reaction rail.
3. Lightweight maglev car.
4. Linear motor fixed to car.
5. Steel suspension rails.
6. Electromagnets.

passengers a fine view. There are 18 monorail stations, and it takes 30 minutes to travel the full track.

Magnetic Levitation (Maglev)

Maglev cars depend on magnetic lift to make them hover about 15mm *above* a track instead of riding *on* one. This means that there are no moving parts to wear out, no need for track maintenance, and almost no noise.

The maglev car has four pairs of electromagnets that act on steel rails on either side of the T-shaped track. The combined effect is to lift the car and also to steer it round bends. Forward movement and braking are provided by a linear motor – like a normal motor, but with the parts split up and laid out flat. Part of the motor is mounted below the car, the other part is an aluminium reaction rail running down the centre of the track.

The world's first commercial maglev service opened in Birmingham, England in 1984. It shuttles between the city's airport and its international exhibition centre – a distance of 620 metres – in 90 seconds.

Rapid Transit

Most modern cities have severe traffic problems which are aggravated by the fact that most people travel to work at about the same time each day.

Private cars have also increased traffic pollution, traffic jams and pressure on car-parking space. Faced with these problems, more and more large cities have turned to railed vehicles to provide a 'rapid transit' service.

Vehicles on fixed routes laid down on rails do not need the same road space and safety margins as free-ranging road vehicles. So railed vehicles can handle larger numbers of people per hour than any road vehicle.

The fastest way of moving a large crowd is a full-size train on standard-gauge track. But laying proper railway tracks can be expensive, and many people live too far from the stations. So a number of lighter, more flexible kind of city railways have been developed.

The simplest system of all is the tram or streetcar.

Below: Modern trams provide convenient street-level transport in Rotterdam.

Above: Roomy double-decker surburban trains carry commuters in and around Toronto in Canada.

Tram-tracks can be laid straight into a normal roadway so that the tram goes right into the city centre, with frequent stops. However, street trams move more slowly than suburban trains, and hold fewer passengers.

To speed them up, tram-tracks can be separated from other traffic by running along the sides of roads or in a central reservation. They can also be laid in completely separate tracks like a railway, sometimes using underground tunnels or elevated sections. Many cities have gradually modified their street tramway systems, replacing busy overground sections with tunnels and transferring street tram-tracks to roadside reservations in places.

Progressive transport authorities try to combine the advantages of a number of systems. Buses are used on light traffic routes, mostly in the outer suburbs. Street trams provide the backbone of the city's transport system. The metro and suburban trains serve the major trunk routes in and out of the city. Flexible ticket systems let passengers transfer between different forms of transit.

**Above: A reminder of a
grander age, St. Pancras
station in London.**

**Below: This newly-built
Rome station has a large
glassed-in shopping area.**

The Changing Station

One of the biggest buildings in most city centres is a railway station. Some of the most imposing were built a century ago, with high glass roofs supported by lofty iron arches. Paris and London both have a number of very fine stations dating from this time, like the Gare du Nord and St. Pancras.

Many of the early stations had to expand in a haphazard way as extra demands were made on them. Some were in cramped city-centre sites with poor access for road vehicles. At first, some tried to cope with goods traffic as well as passengers. Later, all goods except mail, newspapers and perishables like milk and fish were handled at separate goods stations.

In recent years, completely modern stations, such as the Central Station in Rome, have sometimes been built on the site of an old station. In some cases, however, although the new building may be more efficient it can lack the character of the old one.

Old-fashioned booking halls have tended to be replaced by modern concourses with a great variety of shops, cash machines, fast food stalls, and electronic ticket machines. Modern stations often resemble airports more than the stations of the last century.

Below: Ancient and modern blend together inside New York's Grand Central station.

Computerized Travel

Like other forms of transport, the railways have found computers very useful. In marshalling yards, computers can decode information on freight wagons, automatically switching the points to send each wagon to its correct siding.

In stations, computers often control the display of train arrivals and departures. Computer-controlled machines can allow passengers to reserve their seats and sleepers, or even to buy tickets by credit card, without having to wait for attention from a human booking-clerk.

On the Shinkansen Lines
The Tokaido Shinkansen was the first railway line in the world to transfer signals from the trackside to the driver's cab for the 240 km/h *Bullet Trains*. The Automatic Train Control (ATC) system works out the maximum safe speed for any train at any moment. This speed is displayed in the driver's cab, and should the driver ignore it, the ATC system actually applies the brakes until the speed has dropped.

The Shinkansen General Control Centre in Tokyo watches over the positions of all the *Bullet Trains*. A

computer traffic system called COMTRAC normally controls train routes automatically, changing signals and switching points.

On the TGV Track

The TGVs also travel much too fast for their drivers to react to traditional trackside signals. The whole route is controlled from a single signalling centre. Messages and speed limits are sent along the rails, picked up and decoded by the train and displayed in the driver's cab.

The driver has a mass of automatic fault indicators on his console. Many of these

Above: Electronic controls and displays in the cab of a German driver's train.

are to help him correct faults before they become too serious.

TGV passengers also use computers. As when travelling by air, seat reservations are compulsory, as standing is not allowed. Computer-controlled machines in the stations allow passengers to find out what seats are available right up to a few minutes before the train leaves. If your first choice of accommodation is not available, the system suggests alternatives.

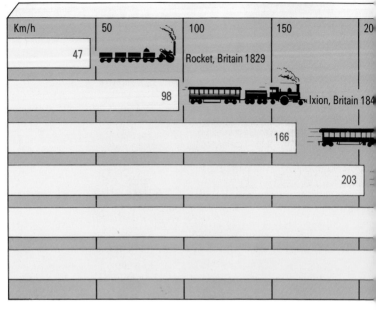

Km/h	50	100	150	20
47		Rocket, Britain 1829		
	98		Ixion, Britain 184	
		166		
			203	

Faster and Faster

Before steam, trains were horse-drawn and slow. The steam engine was the breakthrough that started a steady rise in railway speed records. *Rocket*'s 47km/h at Rainhill in 1829 was beaten the following year by *Northumbrian*'s 58km/h dash to hospital (see page 38).

Throughout the 19th century, record speeds continued to increase. In 1893, the 100mph barrier fell when the New York Central Railroad's '999' claimed 103mph (166km/h). During the next forty years, the record gradually crept up, with many disputes between contenders about how long the speed was sustained, the load being hauled, the gradient and even the weather. *Mallard*'s 1938 run at 203km/h is widely accepted as the record for steam traction.

After World War II, it was the turn of the big French electric locomotives. SNCF held the record in 1953 when engine No. 7121 reached 243km/h. Two years later, No. 7107 beat this by a huge

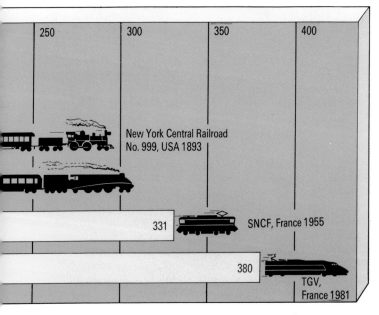

| 250 | 300 | 350 | 400 |

New York Central Railroad
No. 999, USA 1893

331 SNCF, France 1955

380 TGV,
France 1981

margin, sustaining 331 km/h over 2 kilometres. For a quarter of a century this went unchallenged, until in February 1981. TGV No. 16 was timed at 380 km/h on a section of new track.

In the future, new kinds of trains may be developed that could travel at vastly higher speeds, of up to 500 km/h. This could cut inter-city journey times to something like a quarter of their present length. Sheer speed is not always the most important quality in a railway, however. Fast schedules tend to mean fewer stops at stations in between, so that passengers have to use other forms of transport or change trains to reach their destination. Fast journeys also tend to use more fuel, leading to higher fares for passengers.

Nevertheless, modern railways are faced with increasing competition from both sides. The airlines excel at long-haul journeys, and the private car offers great convenience over the short range, often with shorter door-to-door journey times. To defend the middle ground, trains must combine high speed with easy interchange to other forms of transport.

Glossary

Adhesion Ability to grip the rails.

Articulated Hinged or pivoted so that it can bend in the middle.

Axle Metal shaft with wheels at each end.

Banking engine Second engine that joins long-distance trains briefly to help push them up steep hills.

Bogie A frame with two or more axles mounted so that they can turn to follow curves in the track.

Boiler Metal container where water is heated to make steam.

Cab Where the driver sits or stands to control the train.

Class Type of locomotive, often defined by its engine and/or wheel arrangement.

Cutting Section of track where the earth is dug out to avoid a steep gradient.

Diesel Many locomotives use diesel oil as fuel.

Diesel-electrics use generators to drive electric motors that turn the wheels.

Diesel-mechanicals The engine's turning-force is sent directly to the wheels through a gearbox, like a diesel lorry.

Double-heading Hauling a train with two locomotives.

Driving wheels Wheels which are directly powered by the engine. Other wheels (leading and trailing) are just pulled along by the driving wheels.

Duplex Large engine with two sets of driving wheels.

Embankment Section of track where the earth is built up to avoid dips in the track.

Flange Vertical rim attached to a wheel that keeps it running along the inside edge of the rails.

Freight Goods of any kind (as opposed to passengers).

Gauge Distance between the inside edges of the rails. Railways are described as narrow gauge or broad gauge depending on how they compare with the standard gauge of 1.43 metres (4 ft $8\frac{1}{2}$ ins).

Generator Device for producing electricity from a turning force.

Gradient Measure of the steepness of a railway, for example 1 in 30. The ruling gradient of any track is the steepest slope allowable.

Livery Distinctive set of colours, sometimes with special lettering or symbols.

Locomotive The bit that contains engine(s) to pull the train.

Marshalling yard Place where freight wagons are sorted out and arranged into trains with a common destination.

Motor coach Coach with a built-in engine so that it moves by itself (without a separate locomotive).

Multiple unit Set of coaches with a driver's cab at each end and at least one motor coach (containing the engine). Multiple units can be diesel or electric. Several units can be linked up and controlled from the front cab.

Pantograph Metal framework on top of electric trains that collects electricity from overhead wires. It can be lowered when not in use.

Points Lever near a juction that changes the path a train will take.

Rectifier Device for turning alternating electric current (AC) into direct current (DC) so that it is suitable for a train's motors.

Retarder Metal dampers on the rails that slow trucks down when they run over them.

Rolling stock General word for trucks and carriages.

Scale The relationship between a model train and the full-size original on which it is modelled.

Sidings Sections of track not connected to the main line, where rolling-stock can sit until it is needed.

Signal Coloured light (or long movable arm) that tells a driver whether to keep going, slow down or stop.

Sleeper Wooden or concrete support for the track.

Tender The wagon pulled behind a steam locomotive that carries supplies of water and coal for long journeys.

Tram Like a train, a tram is a powered vehicle that runs on rails. If it runs on fenced-off track over long distances, it is called a train. If it mixes with other traffic and runs along roadways, it is called a tram. A tramway is a set of parallel rails or grooves.

Transformer Device for changing the voltage of alternating current (AC) electricity. Electricity is sent along wires at high voltage because this wastes less energy, then stepped down to a lower voltage by transformers on trains.

Wheel arrangement Locomotives are often known by codes showing the number of wheels they have, and whether they are driving wheels or not. A different code is used for diesel and electric engines than for steam engines.

Index

Page numbers in *italics* refer to illustrations

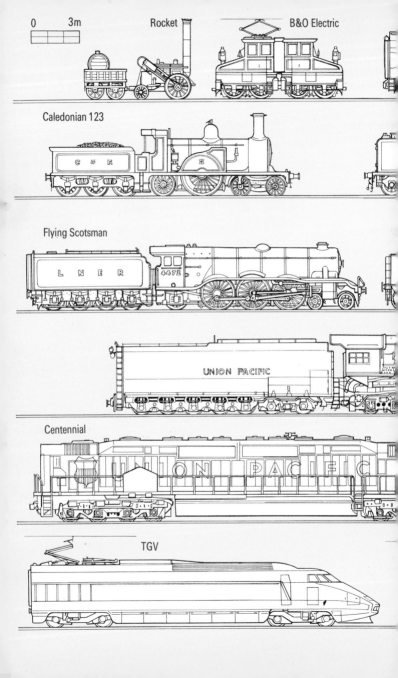

0 3m

Rocket

B&O Electric

Caledonian 123

Flying Scotsman

L N E R 4472

UNION PACIFIC

Centennial

UNION PACIFIC

TGV

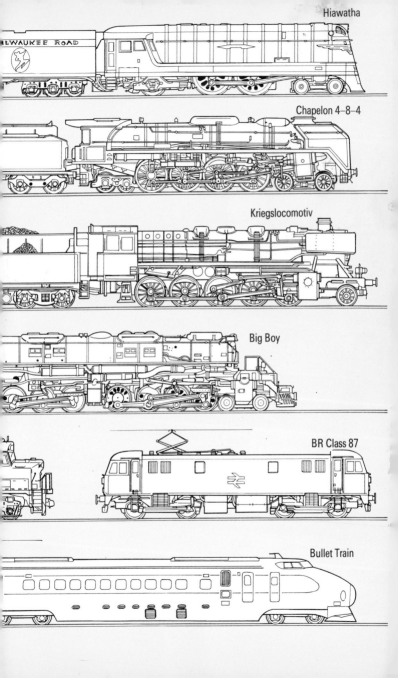

Hiawatha

Chapelon 4–8–4

Kriegslocomotiv

Big Boy

BR Class 87

Bullet Train

Acknowledgments

p12–13 Museum of Transport, Glasgow; p16 Mansell Collection; p19 The Bridgeman Art Library/Royal Holloway College, University of London; p20 (top) Seaboard System Railroad; p27 Colin Garratt; p31 ZEFA; p33 National Railway Museum, York; p37 (top) Japanese National Railways; p39 The Photosource; p44–45 Colin Garratt; p46 Colin Garratt; p48 (top) Greater Manchester Museum of Science and Technology; p50 British Railways Board; p54–55 (top) Japanese National Railways; p54 (bottom) Union Pacific Railroad Museum Collection; p56 Science Museum, London; p57 A.S.E.A.; p58–59 (top) By Courtesy of Bay Area Rapid Transit District; p59 (bottom) Commission de Transport de la Communaute Urbaine de Montreal; p60 Colin Garratt; p61 Colin Garratt; p63 ZEFA; p64 ZEFA; p65 Jacquetta Megarry; p67 Ernst-Paul Lehmann; p68–69 (top) National Library of Ireland, Dublin; p75 Venice Simplon-Orient Express; p76–77 French Railways-Lafontant; p78 Japanese National Railways; p79 Japanese National Railways; p80 Wuppertaler Stadtwerke AG; p81 (middle) GEC Transportation Projects Ltd; p82 M. R. and J. Taplin; p83 Urban Transportation Development Corps; p85 ZEFA; p86 Barclays Bank P.L.C.; p87 Deutsche Bundesbahn; Back cover Colin Garratt.

Picture research: Jackie Cookson.